SHLOMO'S 50 Ways To Save

The Genius Approach to Stretching the Green!

#1

During a party, I offer to place a garbage bin for recycling aluminum cans. Yes, you guessed...all the cans are worth something. Cash in!

#2

When I pump gas, and prices are a little high, I only pump a quarter-tank at a time. Because when I drive down the street a bit, nothing is worse than seeing gas at 10 cents a gallon less, and I filled the tank up with no more room to add the less expensive gas. So, only pump a quarter tank of gas at a time to save money again - the Shlomo way!

#3

Sign up for email coupons or sales from your favorite stores and restaurants. I sign up for every store or restaurant that I like and I always receive coupons or member only sales in my email box. Also, don't forget Digby.com for major alerts on close out products. I bought an 8GB Kingston SD card for only 3.95! Can't beat that!

#4

I always collect extra napkins and condiments when visiting fast food restaurants as I can use them for future use at home-saving money it would cost me to purchase these items retail. Examples: Splenda, Ketchup, Mustard, Mayo, Salt, Pepper, Hot Sauce, Straw, Napkins, mints, toothpicks and etc. Imagine the savings you can have if you just take a little extra next time you eat out.

 # 5

Michael's offers a 50% coupon when you purchase something at regular price. Take this example, you buy a decorative art piece at $50, with the coupon you get 50% off making it $25, but then you can turn around and sell it on Ebay for $60 plus shipping. If you do this, you have made your money back plus $25-now that's Shlomo smarts.

#6

Do the American Consumer Opinion (www.acop.com) online surveys and get paid. This is for real and takes literally no time at all. NO CATCH. Just small trinkets of money. It adds up and in no time you have a couple of hundred dollars. Nice!

#7

Put together gift baskets with items from the dollar store and sell on eBay or other websites. It costs a total of $5 bucks which includes the following: wicker basket, shredded decorative basket paper, shrink wrap for gift basket, coffee and coffee mug. Once completed put it on eBay for $19.99 with free shipping and offer to send to anyone that is on the purchaser's gift giving list. You usually net about $10 bucks after shipping and costs-making you money. Viola!

#8

Get your trees trimmed and ask the tree company to grind the limbs down for mulch and or BBQ wood cooking chips. Then sell them to flea markets, online, or even at garage sales. You can even use them yourself-saving you more money.

#9

Buy an office shredder to cut up your bills, junk mail and etc. Sell the once believed to be garbage as basket fillers, shipping packing material or party confetti.

#10

I often like to save money on my water bill by taking my showers at the gym where I pay a monthly fee. I usually take a long, hot shower without worry of the electricity or water costs since the monthly fee covers the cost. I currently pay $10 a month for my gym. I save over $50 a month doing this. Smart thinking!

#11

Each time I buy Chinese food, I always get a nice Tupperware style food container that my take-out food comes in. Every time I order Chinese, I save on not having to buy these separately from the store. Then, I buy bulk food items such as meat in family packs and freeze in the containers. Thus, saving the costs on food packaging and having ample food frozen for quick weeknight dinners.

#12

Buying in bulk isn't always the answer at some of your local warehouse club stores to save money. But what has worked for me in the past is to buy soft drinks and/or flavored waters with a coupon at these warehouse club stores and then sell them during an event or art show for triple the amount of my cost. One 24 pack of water cost me $2.90 which in turn I sold each bottle for $2.50 making me $60 bucks minus the $2.90 costs and the $30 booth rental per day. I sold over 1000 bottles in a weekend. You do the math....well, I'll help...it netted me about $2320 in two days. Hmmm, most people don't take that home in a week and I made it in one weekend.

#13

Going to the movies? Pack your jacket or purse with all your snacks and drinks. Save money on the high concession stand costs. Remember, a box of Goobers and a soda will set you back close to $10. Eat in style and save money at the same time. Imagine the dollar menu at Taco Bell and what you can have for $10 bucks. A feast! Magnificent!

#14

What kind of place? There is a place I go to when I visit Georgia. They have this meat deal for $20 and you get 20 lbs. of assorted quality meats. I usually buy about 100lbs., place it in a large cooler with dry ice and make my journey back home where the meat is placed in my freezer for at least 6 months worth of food. And all for only a $100! WOW, now that's putting your money where your mouth is.

#15

When you stay in a hotel, resort or motel, you often pay a premium for your stay that is so exaggerated. To get my money's worth, I take the toilet paper, Kleenex and in-room coffee products. On that note, I ask for more of these items by calling the front desk and usually end up getting a week's supply of all items. Saving me moola once again.

#16

Family-style restaurants have been way far the best bargain to date. Get a family style dinning item off the menu, you not only eat like a king while presently there. But you can order more, take a bite, get it boxed and you can eat for the rest of the week. Saves on the groceries and since you have such a diversity of food, it never gets old. Save your green by eating family style!

#17

When eating out, always order a lunch size portion at lunch prices and get the same size meal as if you ordered a dinner entrée. Then you'll have both lunch and dinner wrapped into one.

#18

When ordering out, I often order off of the kid's menu. When ordering to go items, they don't know if I have kids or not. Usually kid's meals are kept cheap to entice parents to buy the more expensive items, but usually the kid's portions are just as big as the adult meal. This can save you up to $10 per entrée.

#19

Wine tastings-most often they cost very little or are free. Just watch for ads in your local paper or online and get one where the wine is flowing and there is catered food. Talk about a cheap night out. I also usually hang out until the tasting is over and get a lot of leftovers that I take home allowing me to eat another day.

#20

During the holidays, I will purchase a gift cards that give bonus gift cards. I then turn around and sell the bonus gift card for $5 less the face value. Then, I take that money and re-invest in more gift cards over and over again until I'm not out of pocket any money...essentially making my meals free.

#21

I go to outlet stores on days when they offer discounts. I often go to a local store where they offer 10% off my purchases. But for each $10 I spend, I get a hole punch on the discount card that they offer. Once I accumulate a full card, I get an additional 20% off in addition to my Friday 10% off discount making for a total of 30% off between the card and the Friday discount. Then, I go to the clearance section where there are items that are usually marked 50% to 80% off. When you add the additional 30% discount, I'm usually ahead of the game or owe just a few cents. I actually walked out with about 7 outfits for a total of $2.18 after all discounts and tax-and they were top brand clothes. Well dressed and smart.

#22

When going to the doctor, I always ask about alternative medicines to the current one I may be taking. The doctor often has sample packs that I can get abundance of-avoiding the prescription costs. Sometimes there are other things better than an apple a day.

#23

I often take friends and family to restaurants to split the check. Often I have a buy one get one free coupon. This equates to 2 paying people in a party of 4. So, if the 2 had total dining charges of $40 dollars, I split these costs and I leave the restaurant spending a whopping $20 for me and my mate. Now that's smart eating.

#24

I frequent home décor stores and look for items that have flaws-especially the ones that are in the clearance section. Once I indentify the flaw, I meet with the manager and make a real low ball offer knowing he or she will rebut with a slightly higher amount. I take it but then turn around and give them a 20% discount coupon that has no restrictions on any item. I get these coupons by just for signing up for their email club. I once left a home décor store paying $45 for a $295 8 ft. silk tree by using this method.

#25

Another way to save at your local home improvement stores is to wait for them to have an item go on sale or clearance. Then, pull out a 10% discount coupon and buy big. Most times, I usually save 50% between the discount coupon and the clearance price by waiting for the sale and using my coupons.

#26

I subscribe to Netflix. It costs me $9.62 a month. I buy popcorn that usually equals out to about a dollar a bag. That's a total of $10.62. I'll then invite a guest for a free movie and popcorn. The only catch is they have to bring a case of beer. In a 2 hour movie, about 12 beers are gone leaving 12 beers in my refrigerator. This means I don't have to spend the money on beer for the next week. Saving me more change for my beer cause.

#27

I always look to buy low and sell high. Well, when I go to conventions or promotional events, I take as many free giveaways that I can. Then I group them together and put them on eBay. I have sold numerous bags, trinkets and whatnots for several dollars only to check my growing balance in Paypal.

#28

There are many times I get a gift or reward from my company. Often, I do not like the item. If I get an item that I do not like, I resell it in a local free newspaper for a good profit. I do this several times a year and when Christmas time comes, I have several hundreds of dollars to be a Super Shlomo Santa.

#29

Oh, the dreaded dental visit. This often can turn into a money saver. After my visit, I grab toothpaste, toothbrushes and dental floss. Not one of each, but about 5 of each. It even expands on my savings when he has the sample mouthwash bottles. Talk about having fresh breath and more change in my pocket. That's putting my money where my mouth is.

#30

When parking in pay metered areas, I always look for a space where someone has the most time left that has recently vacated the spot. This allows me to put minimum change in for the most parking time.

#31

I get my mother to pre-purchase movie tickets on her senior discount. I then buy her discounted tickets and use them myself. Usually at about $3.50 per ticket savings. And, the savings don't stop there. I often take friends with me and they pay me for the full ticket price as I have pre-purchased a ticket for them. I can make about $7 a couple this way. That usually pays for my drink and snack at the movies. Lights, Camera, Action!

#32

Calendars are a wonderful money making dream. Here is what you do. Buy last year calendars with nice looking pictures. Cut the pictures out and put them in frames from the Dollar store. With the cost of the calendar at around $3 and about $1 for each frame, I only have about $1.25 into each piece of framed art. I can then turn around and sell them for $9.99.

#33

Instead of buying fertilizer for my outdoor plants, I set up my own compost consisting of banana peels, cat droppings, tree clippings and leaves. I drop them in a mesh chicken wire container and let them turn into compost before using for my outdoor landscaping. I save tons, while being eco- friendly.

#34

You ever go to a hotel, motel or some type of resort? I know I mentioned earlier that the paper goods are a fair game. But I forgot to point out the soaps, shampoos and in-room coffee. If you travel enough, you'll have a supply that will keep you going clean with diverse types for years to come. (Change to something else, you already mentioned hotel goods.)

#35

Is it cold in your home during the winter months? Want to cut down the energy gulping heat pump/AC unit? To combat this, I put a space heater near the air handler return. It circulates hot air throughout all areas in the home, thus turning an AC system into a turbo heating system. I'm sure you saw the old trick your parents used by turning on the oven to heat an area. Same principle but without the hazard of leaving your oven open.

#36

Collect everyone's information when you meet them. If you ever get into another job that requires some instant leads, you have a nice head start. Believe me, it works. I've used my contacts for everything from fundraisers to sales leads-Even Shlomo's Book of Cheapskate savings.

#37

Dumpster diving is not only for the poor or homeless. It is also for someone looking for some real treasures. Retailers often throw things away just because they are missing pieces and the company they purchased the item from just sends them a replacement. I, for one, have found some nice outdoor furniture for nothing-or almost nothing. All I had to do was buy a couple of bolts, nuts and touch up paint for a real nice backyard addition.

#38

Costco is a cheapskate's dream. Here is the plan. Go there when you are hungry and sample the free food from the sample stations they have set up throughout the whole store. Doesn't cost a thing! Just time and jaw chewing muscles. Eat like a king while you shop the Shlomo way.

#39

Go Trick and Treating even if you are older. Just wear a mask and don't talk. No one will know your age under the mask and by not talking your voice will not give you away. You sure get a lot of goodies to satisfy your sweet tooth without spending a dime doing this. Just don't go as Shlomo, there's only one of me!

#40

Here is a neat one! Go to Universal Orlando Studios and get the Meal Plan! It's only $19.99 for food ALL DAY long... but guess what? You can pack some of the food away in a backpack and have it for the next day or two-another food stretching dollar moment.

#41

The barter system is alive and well. I am sure you have something somebody else wants. Trade it! I have often traded company swag for valuable items. Sometimes, if I get something good in my trade, I put it on eBay for a cash profit.

#42

Good old scratch off lotto tickets. I often get friends and family to go half and half with me so I can limit my losses. If I win, I am honest and split the proceeds. Usually, I get my winnings and stick it in the bank for a couple of weeks, build up some interest, then give them their original half. Doesn't that make cents?

#43

Wait for items at your local grocery store to go on sale to use your coupons. I once got several coupons for Crystal Light at $1.00 off per container. I then waited for my local grocery store to put them on sale. Finally the day arrived, and with their $2.00 instant savings and my $1.00 off, the original $3.55 price was now 55 cents. Wow! What a Shlomo treat.

#44

Always answer surveys from local stores or restaurants. Just keep an eye on your receipts and call the 800 number and you'll get a code to get your free or discounted item. I do and I get free food, merchandise and services from stores or restaurants that I go to anyway.

#45

Buying plants for your home? If they die within a year and they usually do, take the poor plant carcass back to the home improvement store with your receipt and get another plant or your money back. Another great discovery.

#46

I bet you never knew beach sand could bring in some moola. Well, the folks that have never touched beach sand will pay you. How, you ask? Well, simple, bag some up, print a topper to staple to the top of a plastic bag, put it on the internet for $2.00 and viola, you just sold some beach sand. Turn dirt into cash...Shlomo likes this.

#47

Yes, I put the low flow toilets in my house to save on the water bill, but I have taken it one step further, I only flush after a few uses. It's like a 2 for 1 deal for me.

#48

Clip coupons! Then sit on them to wait for the retail to mark down the items then add your coupon for even more savings. I am a coupon clipping machine. I ONLY buy what's on the coupon and most times wait till the item goes on sale. I get double the discount that way. There are many times I get a coupon and hold on to it for a few weeks. Then when the item goes on a sale, then it is Shlomo time to collect. I sometimes wait until the item is Buy One Get One Free before cashing in my coupon for even more savings. I also buy items that go on sale even when I do not need them. Then, I save them for when I do need them. Saving even more money.

#49

I donate my time at fundraisers or volunteer events. Why? Because it is generous and it gets you some free stuff. One time I volunteered at a marathon and received two tickets to a theme park. That was like getting 160 bucks in my pocket for a few hours of time. Doing something good and having a good time-Shlomo thinks this is a great idea!

#50

I buy items **REAL CHEAP** at flea markets and garage sales. I turn around and resell on eBay for twice the price. This usually only works when I buy at the price most wholesalers can buy for. Ebay is Shlomo's heaven on Earth. This is where I can take an item like a vacuum cleaner, buy it for about $20. Then turn around and resell what would have been a $300 vacuum for $99 plus shipping costs. Nothing sucks about this deal.

www.ingramcontent.com/pod-product-compliance
Lightning Source LLC
Chambersburg PA
CBHW051058180526
45172CB00002B/681